The EVERYTHING® Girls

Tons fun kawaii activities— doodles, games, crafts, and more!

Super Cute Kawaii Fun

♥ Book ♥

Peggy Brown and **Nate Lovett**

▲ **adams**media

Avon, Massachusetts

Publisher Karen Cooper

Managing Editor, Everything® Series Lisa Laing

Copy Chief Casey Ebert

Assistant Production Editor Alex Guarco

Acquisitions Editor Pamela Wissman

Associate Development Editor Eileen Mullan

Everything® Series Cover Designer Erin Alexander

An Everything® Series Book.
Everything® and everything.com® are registered trademarks of F+W Media, Inc.

Published by
Adams Media, a division of F+W Media, Inc.
57 Littlefield Street, Avon, MA 02322. U.S.A.
www.adamsmedia.com

ISBN 10: 1-4405-7700-5
ISBN 13: 978-1-4405-7700-0
eISBN 10: 1-4405-7701-3
eISBN 13: 978-1-4405-7701-7

Printed by RR Donnelley, Harrisonburg, VA, U.S.A.

10 9 8 7 6 5 4 3 2 1

June 2014

Many of the designations used by manufacturers and sellers to distinguish their product are claimed as trademarks. Where those designations appear in this book and F+W Media, Inc. was aware of a trademark claim, the designations have been printed with initial capital letters.

Interior illustrations by Nate Lovett.
Cover illustrations by Nate Lovett; © blue67/123RF.

This book is available at quantity discounts for bulk purchases.
For information, please call 1-800-289-0963.

Contents

♡ Acknowledgments ♡

For my super-cute family and happy-go-lucky friends: All the whimsy I put into my work comes from the tons of fun and silliness we've shared together all these years. Each of you occupies an important place in my heart, which giggles with gratitude, and, as you know, is covered in multicolored pompoms and mismatched googly eyes.

Chapter 1

Hey Cuties! What's Kawaii?

Hamsta, Luvva, Oinka, Nananomnom, BeriBeri, Monchacha

"**K**awaii" is a Japanese word that means "cute." Extremely cute. Super cute. Ka-yoot! "Kawaii" pretty much rhymes with "Hawaii," except with just a smidge more emphasis on the last syllable. Ka-why-eee! It even sounds cute. Now you're talkin'!

Pleased to Meet You!

In *The Everything® Girls Super Cute Kawaii Fun Book*, you will get to know this sweet family of Kawaii characters:

Koni, Bunita, Bloomi, Meowy, Kupkaiko, Puffit

Kawaii Is in the Eye-ee of the Beholder

This means that *you* are the one who determines if something is cute enough to be kawaii. Look at something, anything—a character, or a picture, or your brother, and answer these questions:

- Does it smile, and make *me* smile?
- Does it warm *my* heart?
- Does it make *me* want to pick it up, and squeeze it?

If you answered "yes" to any 2 of these questions, smile . . . it's kawaii! Whaddayathink? Which of these do you think are kawaii?

You probably had no problem figuring it out, but here's a clue to whether you picked the kawaii from the rest: *Ace the pooch howls at home runs.*

Kawaii is a word made from 2 Japanese words: *ka*, which means "acceptable," and *ai*, which means "love."

Chapter 2

Good Morning, Bunita!

OFFICIAL
KAWAII CUTENESS
FACTOR METER

Bunita is a bright-eyed, bushy-tailed bunny, with a springy bounce in her step. She's a math whiz, especially with multiplication. If you ask her to figure out how many carrots she'll need to make 3 carrot cakes, she'll hop right on it! Blessed with expert listening skills, Bunita loves to eavesdrop, and even though she lives in a tangled briar patch, she never has a hare out of place. If you catch up to her, rub her feet—they're lucky!

Funnybunny Jokes

When Bunita gets married, where will she go after the wedding?
On her bunnymoon

What game does Bunita like to play on the playground?
Hopscotch!

How do you catch an unusual bunny like Bunita? *Unique up on her!*

What airline does Bunita fly when she goes to London? *British Hare-ways!*

Where does Bunita work? *At the I-HOP!*

Snack Attack!

Besides carrot cake, Bunita enjoys chomping on cute lettuce wraps from tropical islands. Here's her favorite secret recipe.

Bunita's Kawaiian Hawaiian Lettuce Wraps

Romaine or Boston lettuce leaves
Dijon mustard, mayonnaise, or a mixture of both
Thinly sliced ham
Shredded mozzarella cheese
Pineapple tidbits

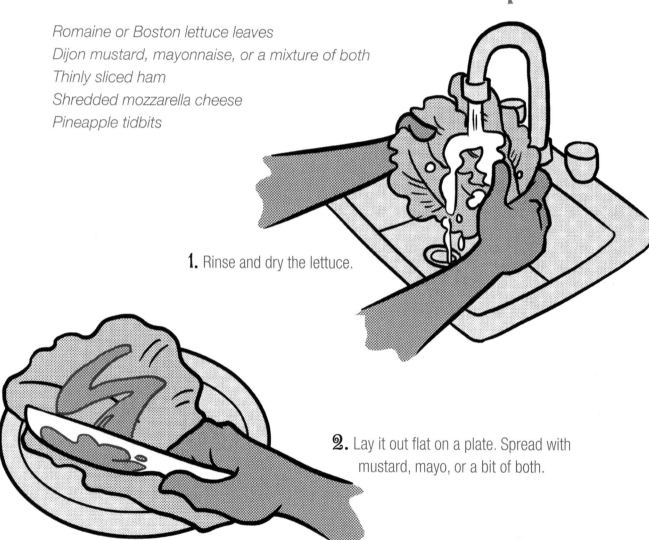

1. Rinse and dry the lettuce.

2. Lay it out flat on a plate. Spread with mustard, mayo, or a bit of both.

3. On top of that, lay down a little ham, a few cheese shreds, and some pineapple tidbits.

4. Roll the whole thing all the way up, and then munch it all the way down!

Carrot Cake Caper

Even though Bunita enjoys those lettuce wraps, sometimes she's just gotta have a slice of sweet and scrumptious carrot cake. Help her find her way from the briar patch to the Garden Gate Café.

Hello there! Hello Kitty is a world-famous kawaii character—even more famous than Bunita. At least for now.

Chapter 3

Heeere's Koni!

Some think he's cold, but really he's just plain cool. Koni is a total sweetie who is quick to make friends because he always knows the scoop. He hails from Alaska where winter is his favorite season, and he excels in sundae school. Though he's got a crunchy exterior, Koni can be a real softie once he gets warmed up. His personality is a mix of Peanut Butter Punch, Silliness Ripple, Prickly Pineapple, and Laughing Lemon, and if you get in a fight with Koni, watch out! You're the one who's gonna get licked!

I Scream for Ice Cream Jokes!

Where did Koni learn his ABCs?
At sundae school.

How does Koni communicate
with his friends?
He has a cell cone.

What gymnastic move is popular
with ice creams all over the world?
Banana Splits

Of what heritage is
Koni's family?
They're Neapolitan.

Why did Koni lose his
job at the bank?
He was double-dipping.

Koni's Flavor Forecast

Find these flavors in the flurry:

BANANA

BING CHERRY

BLUEBERRY

BUTTER BRICKLE

BUTTERSCOTCH

CARAMEL

CHOCOLATE

CINNAMON

COOKIE DOUGH

KIWI

LEMON

NEAPOLITAN

PEACH

PEPPERMINT

PINEAPPLE

ROCKY ROAD

ROOT BEER

SPUMONI

STRAWBERRY

VANILLA

E	I	V	W	T	C	C	O	O	K	I	E	D	O	U	G	H	V	C
L	X	N	J	A	I	E	I	I	D	O	I	V	A	N	I	L	L	A
P	B	E	S	N	J	T	G	L	Y	R	R	E	H	C	G	N	I	B
P	M	B	C	A	B	A	M	E	C	V	Q	J	P	N	C	O	U	J
A	T	X	I	N	F	L	T	M	D	F	D	H	N	Z	R	J	S	Y
E	T	L	N	A	N	O	O	A	G	C	C	A	K	O	E	E	L	Q
N	P	Z	N	B	B	C	N	R	S	T	T	S	C	B	E	O	T	K
I	T	K	A	E	L	O	T	A	O	I	G	K	S	U	R	K	N	B
P	I	L	M	L	P	H	Z	C	L	J	Y	Z	P	T	E	I	I	W
E	H	W	O	G	E	C	S	O	K	R	P	Y	U	T	E	W	M	O
I	U	X	N	B	F	R	P	U	O	Z	R	P	M	E	B	I	R	Y
H	U	C	H	Y	E	A	Q	A	Q	R	Z	X	O	R	T	F	E	R
Y	C	A	S	T	E	K	D	H	E	B	V	J	N	B	O	N	P	R
K	Z	G	T	N	H	J	R	B	B	N	T	C	I	R	O	I	P	E
Z	Q	U	N	K	O	C	W	X	E	Z	O	N	R	I	R	E	E	B
X	B	C	B	D	D	A	A	X	F	S	B	M	R	C	I	C	P	E
L	H	D	X	Y	R	U	X	E	J	A	Y	E	E	K	T	H	L	U
R	X	S	M	T	O	N	T	U	P	U	Z	J	F	L	F	N	E	L
B	K	X	S	Y	H	G	B	N	M	U	W	Q	S	E	D	G	E	B

Kawaiice Cream Cone

Draw something cute and lovable or write the name of somebody you love in each of the little waffle squares of Koni's crunchy cone. Maybe you'll even melt his heart!

Koni is a good example of anthropomorphism (AN-throw-poh-MORF-ism), which is when things and objects that aren't alive are given human qualities. Actual ice cream cones can't smile, but Koni is an anthropomorphic kawaii character, so he can. He might also wink at you when you're not looking.

Oinka is the cleanest piggy in the pen, because mud, slop, and wallowing simply aren't cute. Oinking, on the other hoof, is very cute, especially when you giggle between oinks the way Oinka does. Despite the fact that she is a sweet and proper piglet, Oinka thinks bacon jokes are funny, and she pokes fun at her friends with her curlicue tail. Though you will never catch her eating a ham sandwich, Oinka is a big fan of every other kind of sandwich, and likes to cuddle like a pig in a blanket.

Piggly Gigglies

Why can't Oinka keep a secret?
She can't control herself—she squeals!

How does Oinka like to wear her hair?
In pigtails

What is Oinka's favorite ballet?
Swine Lake

Why does Oinka want to become an actress? *Because she's a ham!*

What karate moves does Oinka like to do most? *Pork chops*

What is Oinka doing if she has cookies in the oven? *She's bacon.*

Sunshine and Lollipops

When things are going well, and Oinka is happy, you could say her outlook is all sunshine and lollipops! Use the kawaii-clues to fill in the blanks of this perky piggy's puzzle.

ACROSS

3. Worthy of adoration

6.  -able

7. What this makes you

8. One of these makes you . . .

9. Rhymes with MOVIE

11. Go out and play in the . . .

12.

DOWN

1.

2.  is . . .

4. Cherry, grape, or apple?

5. There is no other word for this pure enjoyment . . .

8. Describe this in one word:

10. Looking beautiful

Create Kawaii Characters

Creating kawaii characters is simple-schmimple! Just put a very cute smile on your face and follow these guidelines to learn to draw Oinka, and then use your kawaii technique on your own paper to draw Koni, Bunita, and your own original cuties.

There are a lot of famous pigs: Porky Pig, Miss Piggy, Piglet, Babe, Pumbaa, the Three Little Pigs, Wilbur, and, of course, Oinka. Oinka is the kawaii-est of them all!

1.

2.

3.

4.

5.

Pompom Pals

Whether you produce a piggy, or prefer to manufacture a monster, pompom pals are definitely considered kawaii, because no matter what you make, they're super-cute!

Stuff you need from the craft store:

Glue
Pompoms of various sizes and colors
Scissors
Felt or fun foam of various sizes and colors
Googly eyes of various sizes

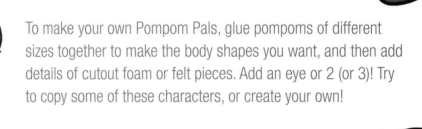

To make your own Pompom Pals, glue pompoms of different sizes together to make the body shapes you want, and then add details of cutout foam or felt pieces. Add an eye or 2 (or 3)! Try to copy some of these characters, or create your own!

You can't make a mistake on your Pompom Pals no matter what, because anything that's fuzzy and has googly eyes is automatically cute!

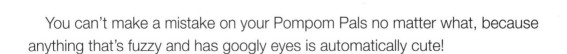

Luvva Who? Luvva You!

OFFICIAL
KAWAII CUTENESS
FACTOR METER

Luvva is a heart with soul. Happy and always in love, Luvva can keep the beat to any song, and will dance to music all night long. Her favorite color is red, her favorite candy is chocolate, her favorite flowers are roses, her favorite holiday . . . Halloween! (What? You thought it would be Valentine's Day?) Often unpredictable, Luvva is very delicate and sometimes gets broken, but she never stops ticking!

Heart Ack-Acks to Make You Laugh

Knock-Knock
Who's there?
Olive.
Olive who?
Olive YOU!

What do you call it
when Luvva mumbles?
A heart murmur

Luvva: Let's run away and get married!
Melon: I love you, but I Cantaloupe!

Valentine's Day is the heart holiday.
What's the holiday for milk?
Gallon-tine's Day!

The heart shape as you know it is an *ideograph*—a symbol that represents an idea—in this case, the idea of love. People have used the heart shape as a symbol of love for over 700 years.

What does Luvva wear when it's raining?
A vein-coat!

Doodle Art You Know by Heart

What's a doodle? A doodle can be anything you like. Start with a heart and let your pen go! Here are some examples and inspiration to get you going. It's up to you to fill in all the blank spaces with oodles of doodles.

F.I.B. Love Story

Do you know what an F.I.B. story is? It's a story *you* help write by Filling In (the) Blanks. So go for it! Ask your friends to give you random words to fill in the blanks before you actually read the story. Then read it aloud to all your contributors. It's a laugh and a half!

The _____ Heart
Adjective

It was a _____ and _____ night, but love was in the air.
adjective   adjective

BeriBeri and her boyfriend _____ were enjoying a delightful _____
boy's name   food

dinner by candlelight. There was a knock at the door. _____ went
Same boy's name

to answer it, but no one was there. They went back to their dinner, and dined on

baskets of _____, _____ bowls of _____, and glasses of
food   adjective   food

_____, which smelled like _____.
drink   something smelly

Again, there was a knock at the door, or what sounded like a _____
adjective

thud, thud, thud. This time BeriBeri went to answer it, and again, nobody was there.

The wind blew, and _____ and _____ came in the windows as the
plural noun   plural noun

storm _____ grew stronger. Crack! Thud! _____! _____! _____!
adverb   Noise   Noise   Noise

Up from a loose floorboard popped Luvva—and you could hear her heart thumping!

"Sorry to interrupt your _____ date!" she shouted. I got stuck in there
adjective

after I slipped on a _____ and fell on my _____! I guess I better
noun   body part

take my _____ heart and beat it!"
adjective from the title

Chapter 6

BeriBeri Is Very Very Sweet

OFFICIAL
KAWAII CUTENESS
FACTOR METER

Not just another cute face, BeriBeri is one smart cookie. Okay, she's not a cookie, but you get the idea. BeriBeri is anything but boring. Her interests range from chemistry to rocket science to fruit-basket weaving. Her boyfriend is Toast, but she has an occasional crush on Shortcake. She's sweet, blushes easily, and wears the most adorable little green cap. Because of her smarts, she rarely finds herself in a jam.

Strawberry Snickers

Which *Wizard of Oz* character loves strawberries?
The Scarecrow

Use 2 words to describe strawberry frozen yogurt.
Berry cold

What do you call 150 strawberries bunched together?
A strawberry jam

What did the strawberry
say on December 25?
Berry Christmas!

Tutti Fruity Duty

Find the fruits in this field!

 APPLE

 NECTARINE

BANANA

ORANGE

CANTALOUPE

PEACH

GRAPES

 PLUM

HONEYDEW

POMEGRANATE

KIWI

STRAWBERRY

 LEMON

TANGERINE

LIME

WATERMELON

Y	T	C	I	J	J	U	B	P	W	N	G	G	N	M
J	R	A	P	Z	K	Q	L	V	O	E	E	N	O	R
S	A	R	N	D	D	U	M	M	E	R	L	B	L	C
U	E	Q	E	G	M	W	E	N	U	I	P	L	E	K
P	R	P	U	B	E	L	I	T	O	X	P	I	M	X
J	J	D	A	S	W	R	V	Q	R	H	A	M	R	E
K	A	H	B	R	A	A	I	C	O	O	D	E	E	J
Y	I	P	G	T	G	L	R	N	N	N	U	I	T	V
G	O	W	C	M	B	D	D	T	E	E	R	A	A	W
V	Z	E	I	A	B	E	Z	K	S	Y	I	B	W	U
G	N	N	E	G	N	A	R	O	D	P	T	Q	U	
X	X	A	I	H	R	B	W	G	O	E	I	N	D	M
A	N	D	D	P	E	A	C	H	G	W	V	S	T	M
A	X	E	T	A	N	A	R	G	E	M	O	P	L	Z
C	A	N	T	A	L	O	U	P	E	P	B	G	Y	I

A Berry Reflective Poetry Collection

Flip your brain and see if you can read these poems. If you can't, hold them up to a mirror and it'll flip them for you.

Roses are red,
Violets are blue,
Strawberries are sweet,
And owls say, "Whoo."

There once was a berry named Fred,
With seeds all over his head.
He babbled a lot:
"Bip boopity bot,"
And nobody knows what he said.

Sweet strawberries in a dish . . .
How many berries do you wish?

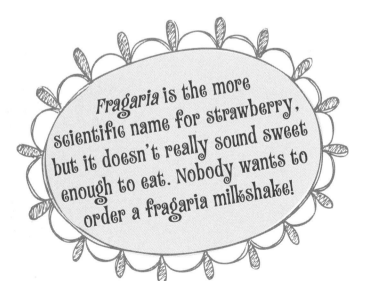

Fragaria is the more scientific name for strawberry, but it doesn't really sound sweet enough to eat. Nobody wants to order a fragaria milkshake!

Nananomnom:
Short for
Bananananananomnomnom,
Is Long on Talent

Delicious and endlessly ap-peel-ing, Nanan-omnom, or Nana for short, is a famous dancer from Central America. She knows the waltz and the twist, but prefers to groove in bunches while doing the monkey and the splits. Flamenco guitar is her passion, and she's renowned for her influence over corn flakes. Her Latin guitar playing has made her famous in clubs the world over, but when daylight comes, she wan' go home.

Nananomnom: Short for Banananananananomnomnom, Is Long on Talent 53

Funana Nyuk-Nyuks

Why did Cindernana wear 2 banana peels on her feet to the ball?
She needed a pair of slippers!

What's yellow on the inside and brown and fuzzy on the outside?
A banana in a monkey suit!

Time flies like a bird,
but fruit flies like a banana.

Why did Nananomnom
go out with a prune?
*Because she couldn't
find a date.*

What do you call the
noontime meal eaten by
a group of bananas?
Bunch lunch

Nananomnom: Short for Banananananomnomnom, Is Long on Talent   55

Make Thumbody Thpecial

Do you have thumbs? Great! Then you can make Thumbprint Buddies! Take washable markers and color your thumbprints, then stamp them onto paper and draw on cute faces, arms, legs, and other details! You can make cute scenes and write even cuter stories. You are a thumbs-up kawaii artist!

Fingerprints and thumbprints
are made up of "friction ridges,"
which actually help us grip things,
especially when our hands are wet.
Adding happy faces to them
is completely kawaii.

Draw Nananomnom!

Creating more kawaii characters is easy-peasy! First draw Nana, and then use your kawaii technique on your own paper to draw Luvva, BeriBeri, and your own original cuties.

All 47 Japanese prefectures, which are kind of like states or provinces in Japan, have their own super-cute mascot character. For example, Kumamoto Prefecture has a cute mascot named Kumamon, who is a happy, roly-poly, black, bear-like character with rosy red cheeks.

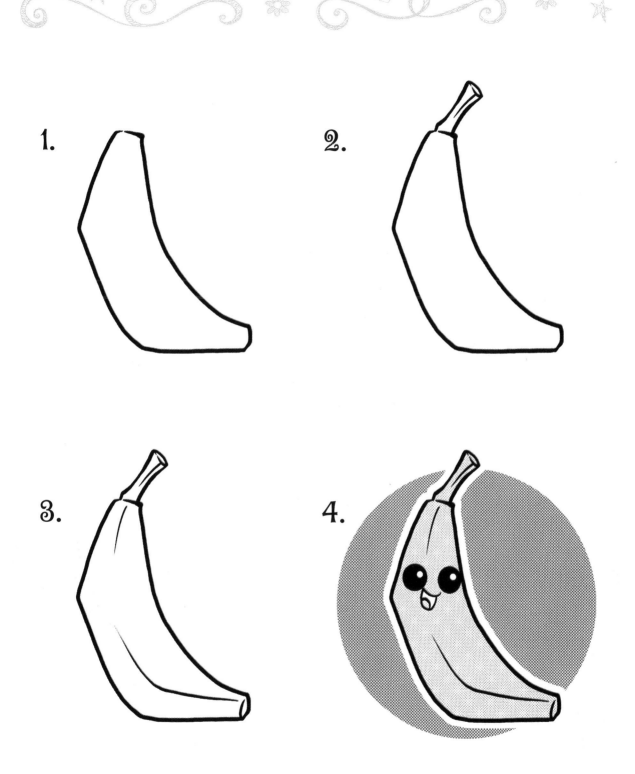

1.

2.

3.

4.

Nananomnom: Short for Bananananananomnomnom, Is Long on Talent   59

Code Cracker

Use the following key to crack the code and uncover a bit of somewhat spotty banana wisdom.

A	B	C	D	E	F	G	H	I
1	2	3	4	5	6	7	8	9

J	K	L	M	N	O	P	Q	R
10	11	12	13	14	15	16	17	18

S	T	U	V	W	X	Y	Z
19	20	21	22	23	24	25	26

‾1 ‾2 ‾1 ‾14 ‾1 ‾14 ‾1   ‾23 ‾9 ‾20 ‾8   ‾19 ‾16 ‾5 ‾3 ‾11 ‾12 ‾5 ‾19   ‾9 ‾19

‾19 ‾1 ‾9 ‾4   ‾20 ‾15   ‾8 ‾1 ‾22 ‾5   ‾6 ‾18 ‾5 ‾3 ‾11 ‾12 ‾5 ‾19.

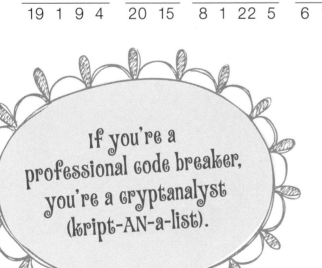

If you're a professional code breaker, you're a cryptanalyst (kript-AN-a-list).

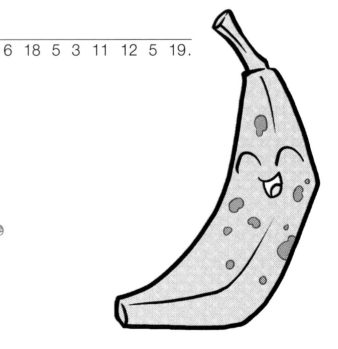

Chapter 8

Meowy Is the Cat's Pajamas

OFFICIAL
KAWAII CUTENESS
FACTOR METER

Originally from France, Meowy is stylish and cool in her fashionable fur coat. She becomes fast friends with everybody, and she's popular because she's curious and always up for anything. When she's not skydiving or parasailing, Meowy likes to purr and stretch out in the afternoon sun. She's a finicky French feline for sure. Even though she adores tuna salad and ice cream bars, if you offer them to her, she'll quietly walk away.

Finicky Funnies

What do you call a cat that likes atomic sourballs?
Sour puss

How does Meowy like to shop?
From a cat-alog

Where does Meowy hear the latest headlines?
On the evening mews

What does Meowy eat for breakfast?
Mice Krispies

What happened when a cat swallowed a ball of yarn?
She had mittens!

A domestic cat can sprint at almost 30 miles per hour. That's feline-fast! But so far, no cats have gotten speeding tickets for running through the kitchen.

Meowy Muffins

Try these yummy Meowy Muffins for breakfast or lunch. You'll need:

1 English muffin
1 slice of bread
Smooth peanut butter or chocolate hazelnut spread
4 raisins
2 small candy-coated chocolate candies
Pretzel sticks

1. Split the English muffin in half.

2. Toast both halves, along with the bread.

3. Cut the 4 corners off the toasted bread.

4. Add the bread corners to the round muffin halves to form cat ears using peanut butter like glue.

5. Slather the English muffin halves with peanut butter or chocolate-hazelnut spread.

6. Make a face using raisins for eyes, a piece of candy for a nose, and pretzel sticks for whiskers.

7. Smile! Breakfast is ready!

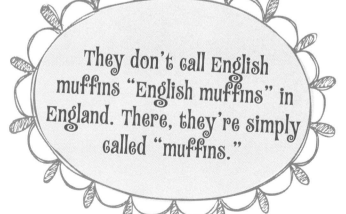

They don't call English muffins "English muffins" in England. There, they're simply called "muffins."

Kitten Caboodle

You can make a caboodle of kittens with a clump of clay and a pointy pencil!

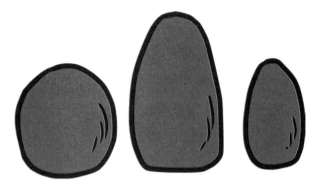

1. First make a bunch of clay balls—they can be perfectly round, a bit egg-shaped, or even more hot-dog shaped.

2. Once you have them ready, pinch 2 little ears at the top.

3. Poke them with the point of the pencil to make eyes, nose, and mouth. Simple!

4. Depending on what kind of clay you have, you might be able to let them air-dry and color them with markers, or they might require baking. Check the clay package for instructions.

Share your kitties with your buddies!

Chapter 9

Bloomi Stops to Smell the Roses

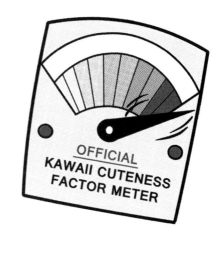

OFFICIAL
KAWAII CUTENESS
FACTOR METER

Not your typical petal pusher, Bloomi is calm and cool, and she takes time to enjoy the finer things in life. She doesn't like to travel, so she put down roots right where she grew up. On occasion, if insulted, she'll come back with a thorny remark, but in general, no other kawaii character acts (or smells) as sweet. Bloomi's favorite holiday is Mother's Day, because she gets to make people smile, hang out with a bunch of friends, and ride along in the florist's truck on the delivery route.

Garden Giggles

What does Bloomi's mom
say to her each morning?
'Morning, Glory!

What kind of flowers
grow on your face?
Tulips!

How might you say that a beautiful flower got up in the morning?
A rose arose

What kind of pickles do flowers like?
Daffo-dills

If April showers bring May flowers, what do May flowers bring?
Pilgrims!

Friends Forever Forget-Me-Nots

What's your favorite thing about your best friend? Can't narrow it down to just one thing? Lucky you! Get together with your BFF and make FFFMNs (Friends Forever Forget-Me-Nots), to make sure you'll stay best friends forever.

Materials you'll need:

Scissors
Colored or printed paper or fabric scraps
Plain sheets of paper
Glue
Buttons
Pencil, pen, or marker

Awww! The forget-me-not is a sweet little flower. Its scientific name is *Myosotis*, which means "mouse's ear" in Greek, which is almost as cute as "Forget-me-not."

1. Cut some petals from the colored paper or fabric scraps. Arrange them on a piece of plain paper in a flower-like fashion. Glue them down on the paper, but put glue only at the inside edges of the petals, so that they can be lifted up by their tips later.

2. Cut a circle of a different color from colored paper or fabric, and glue that down in the middle of the petals.

3. Glue a button on top of the centerpiece of your flower.

4. Lift each petal, and write something that you really like about your friend. Write it very tiny on the paper underneath the petal. Make it so that when you put the petal back down, your writing is hidden.

5. When you're both done, trade flowers.

Zigzag Garden

How does your garden grow? All zigzag? Yes!
Filled with blooming Bloomi blooms? Absolutely!

Materials you'll need:

Cereal box or other cardboard
Scissors
Glue
Green pipe cleaners

Some or all of the following: markers,
paints, craft foam, different colored pipe
cleaners, colored paper, felt, fabric scraps.
Scented body spray or perfume

1. Open up an empty cereal box, and cut a long strip from it about 3 or 4 inches wide, and as long as can be. Then fold the strip into a zigzag so it will stand up on its own.

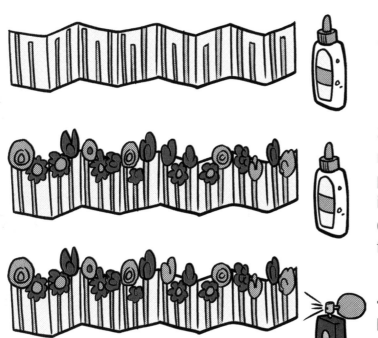

2. Glue a pipe cleaner in the center of each fold in the cardboard.

3. Use your art supplies and fabric scraps to make all kinds of flower blossoms, some you've probably already seen, and some that only occur in your imagination. Glue the flower blooms on top of the stems, so they stick up over the top edge of the zigzag base.

4. Spray a little body spray or perfume onto the blooms for a flowery aromatic effect.

Tah-dah! Stop and smell the roses! Or petunias . . . or chrysanthemaisies . . .

Chapter 10

Kupkaiko Saves the Day

OFFICIAL
KAWAII CUTENESS
FACTOR METER

Faster than a rolling doughnut! Able to leap tall layer cakes in a single bound! It's a brownie! It's a muffin! No! It's Kupkaiko! Ever meet a superhero cupcake before? Well, now you have. Kupkaiko is a model citizen who's always on call to cake-pop over to help any victims of injustice. Kupkaiko always behaves like angel food rather than devil's food, and his double spongy superlayers with fierce frosting and power sprinkles give him the might to do what's right!

Cake Crackups

Why did the kid eat
her homework?
*She said it was a
piece of cake.*

What is an elf's
favorite kind of cake?
Shortcake

Why did Kupkaiko go to the doctor?
He was feeling crummy.

How, exactly, was Kupkaiko feeling crummy?
He had a stomach-cake!

What do you get from a shaky baker?
A cake quake

Cupcake Carnations

Make a sweet bouquet for somebody sweet!

Materials you'll need:

Cupcake wrappers in different colors
Pipe cleaners
Glue
Scissors

Cupcakes are awesome. If you go to Sydney, Australia, and want to order one, call it a "patty cake," and if you're in London, ask for a "fairy cake." No matter where you go, they're cute and cakeylicious!

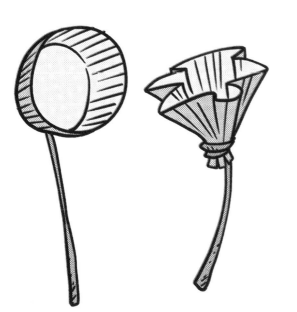

1. Layer and twist cupcake wrappers of various colors to make flowery blooms.

2. Take a pipe cleaner and twist it around part of your bloom, or glue it to the back of your bloom to form a stem.

3. Cut some of the wrappers to make petals of different shapes too. You can even string a garland of cupcake wrapper flowers.

There is no right way to make these, and just like in nature, every single flower will be different!

Draw Kupkaiko!

Sharpen your pencil and prepare to draw! Follow these guidelines to learn to draw Kupkaiko, and then use your kawaii technique on your own paper to draw Meowy, Bloomi, and your own original cuties.

1.

2.

3.

4.

Chocolate Kupkaiko Cake in a Mug

Ask your parents if you can make this together—it's easy, but it's hot! And it's too delicious not to share.

4 tablespoons sugar

4 tablespoons flour

1½ tablespoons cocoa

1 large egg, beaten

3 tablespoons vegetable oil

3 tablespoons milk

½ teaspoon vanilla

3 tablespoons chocolate morsels

1. Place all ingredients in a very large microwave-safe mug.

2. Mix really well with a fork.

3. Microwave on high for 2 minutes and 30 seconds. Whoa! While it's cooking, the cake may rise up above the top edge of the mug. But don't worry. It'll be okay. Really!

4. When time's up, cake is ready! Let it cool off so you don't burn your tongue!

Mmmmmmmm!

Chapter 11

Monchacha
the Magical
Merry Monster

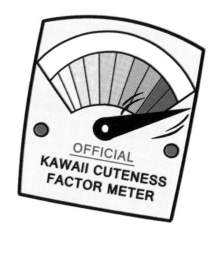

OFFICIAL
KAWAII CUTENESS
FACTOR METER

Monsters can be scary. And ugly. And mean. But not Monchacha. Monchacha is a funny, fuzzy, friendly monster with a contagious laugh and a pocket full of fun. Need a bouncy ball? Ask Monchacha. Need a jump rope, a yoyo, a snowball, a fish tank, a pizza, or a roller coaster? Monchacha has it all in her magical polka-dot pockets, and she loves to share. She's not scary . . . she's Monchacha—the happiest, kindest monster ever!

Monchacha the Magical Merry Monster   89

Monchacha-ha-ha!

What do you say to
a 2-headed monster?
Hello, hello!

What does a really
big monster drive?
A monster truck

What do monsters
use to keep cool in
the summertime?
A scare-conditioner

What's a monster's favorite thing at the playground?
The scary-go-round

Why did Monchacha cross the playground?
To get to the other slide

Jim Henson created the Muppets, many of which are monsters, and many of which are cute!

Rock Monstaaaaah!

Ever been to a rock concert? Ever put on a rock concert? Here's your chance!
Get rockin'!

You will need:

Paints and paintbrushes
Small rocks of various shapes and sizes
Markers
Glue
Googly eyes

Pictographs and petroglyphs are both kinds of rock art that date way back to prehistoric times. By decorating cute rocks with cute faces, you're making a kawaii-glyph. We just made up that word!

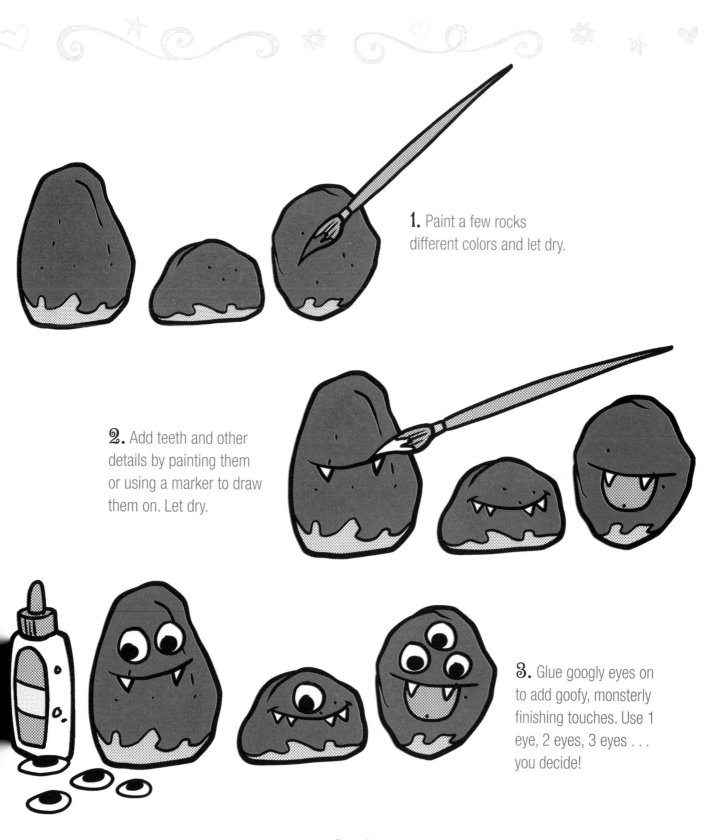

1. Paint a few rocks different colors and let dry.

2. Add teeth and other details by painting them or using a marker to draw them on. Let dry.

3. Glue googly eyes on to add goofy, monsterly finishing touches. Use 1 eye, 2 eyes, 3 eyes . . . you decide!

Monchacha the Magical Merry Monster 93

Clueless Crossword Cruzzle

Monchacha doesn't have a clue, and neither do you! But since she and some of her monster friends have filled their weird names in all the down spots, it's up to you to fill the rest of these monster names in all the across spots.

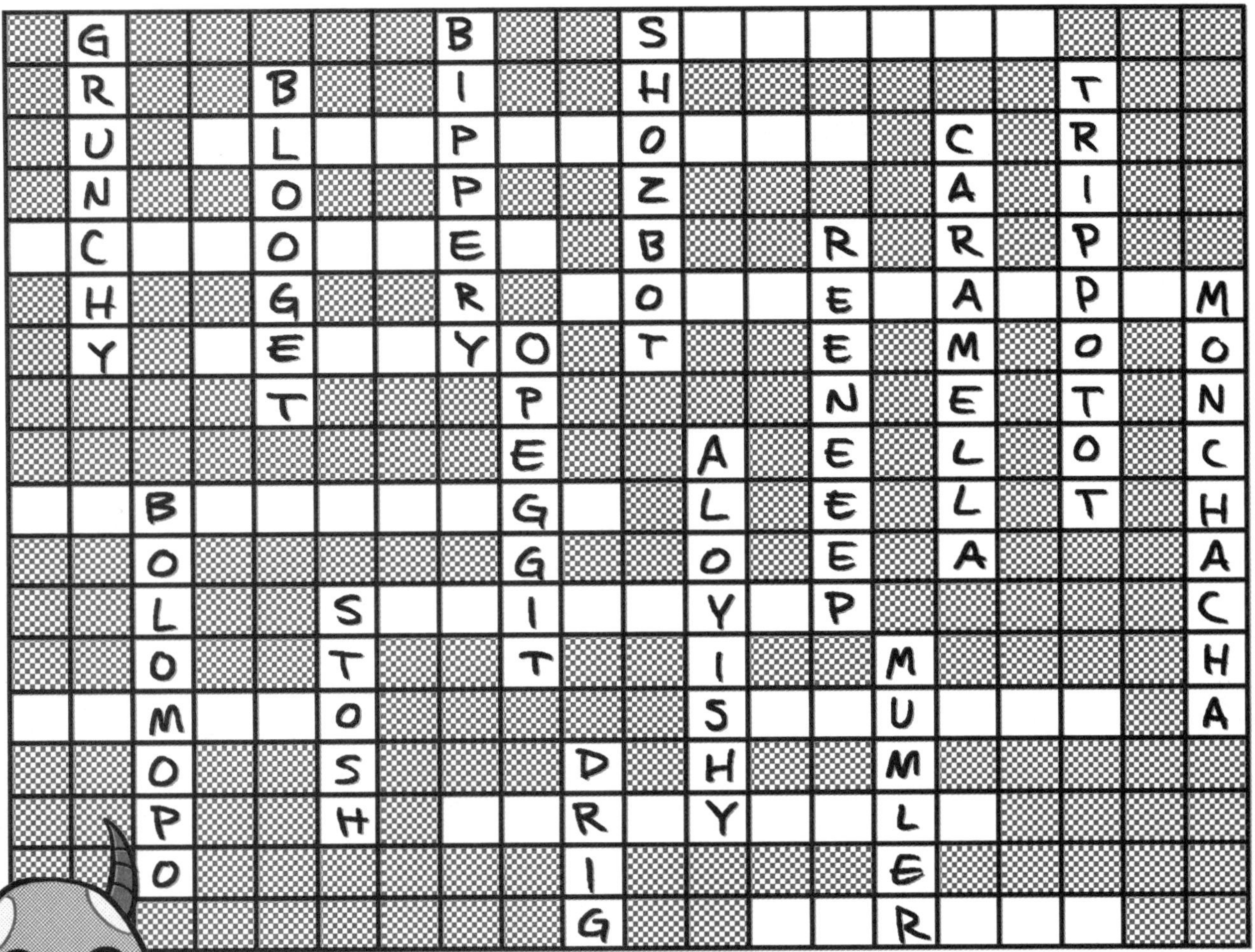

Goreki
Squiddyup
Gooberappom
Klimperooni

Smunkey
Jabberelga
Schmooper
Mellyo

Shlunky
Purpyella
Hamboo

Chapter 12

Hamsta Runs a Marathon: Doesn't Go Far

OFFICIAL
KAWAII CUTENESS
FACTOR METER

Handier than your average gerbil, Hamsta rigged his hamster wheel with an odometer to keep track of how many miles he's already run without really getting anywhere. Hamsta also managed to connect his wheel to a generator, which now powers his giant boom box, a smoothie blender, a massage chair, and a hamster-sized video game arcade. Clearly, Hamsta has other interests than running, and he looks forward to playing with his custom toys . . . if ever he stops running around. And around. And around!

Hamsta-laffsta

Where do European hamsters come from?
Hamsterdam

Why did the teacher like Hamsta so much?
He's the teacher's pet.

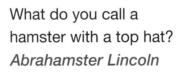

What do you call a hamster with a top hat?
Abrahamster Lincoln

Why doesn't Hamsta ever
tell a bedtime story?
He doesn't have a tale!

Why did Hamsta return the
gift he got for his birthday?
He already has a fur coat.

The Angora hamster
is also known as the teddy
bear hamster, which is
almost too cute to even
think about.

Snowball the Hamster

Snack cakes are yummy and hamsters are funny, and hamsters made of snack cakes are funny-yummy.

Chewy fruit-flavored square candies (like Starburst)
Frosting in a tube
Jellybeans or little round candies
Twinkies, coconut Sno Balls, or other little snack cakes
Dry spaghetti noodles

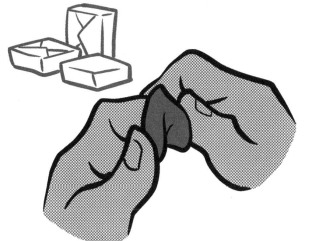

1. Use the chewy fruit square like a piece of clay . . . knead it until you can shape bits of it into ears.

2. Use the frosting like glue to stick the ears, candy eyes, and jellybean nose on to the snack cakes, and then break pieces of spaghetti and stick them into the cake like skinny little whiskers.

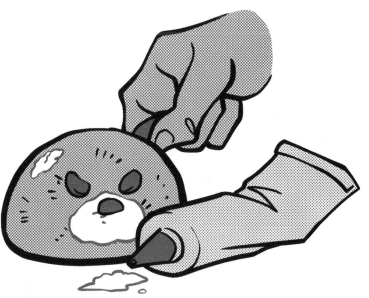

3. Sniffsniff . . . you've created a Hamsta!

Have a Hamster Ball!

Now Hamsta can get off the wheel and get on the ball! You will need:

Scissors
Felt scraps
Glue

1 big pompom
1 tiny pompom
Clear plastic holiday ornament ball
that comes apart in 2 halves

1. Cut little ears and eyes out of felt, and glue them to the big pompom.

2. Glue the tiny pompom on in nose-position. Voilà! Hamsta!

3. Place Hamsta gently inside the clear ball.

4. Squeak, "Holy hamsters!" It's sooo kawaii!

There is a video game called *HamsterBall* where players try to control a hamster in a ball through obstacles that stand in the way of its favorite food.

Chapter 13

Puffit
Is Heaven-Scent

Most clouds are made of water vapor, but Puffit is made of something better—a clump of heavenly mist that smells like freshly baked chocolate chip cookies! When she floats past you, your mouth will water and you'll pour yourself a glass of milk. Puffit is a shape-shifter; she can puff up like a cotton ball, drift into a dinosaur, lengthen like a banana, and glide into a Godzilla-shaped glob. She can rain on demand, but loves to let the sun shine through and help make rainbows whenever she can.

Cloudy Comedy

What did one raindrop
say to the other?
*Two's company, three's
a cloud!*

What does Puffit wear
underneath her puffy exterior?
Thunderwear!

When clouds and wind
play together, what's
their favorite game?
Twister!

What should you ask Puffit if she jokes around an awful lot? *Are you cirrus?*

What day is it when Puffit and her cloud friends decide not to come out? *Sunday!*

There are lots of different types of clouds. The main types are stratus, cirrus, and cumulus. Stratus clouds are flat. They look like layers of sheets or thin blankets. Cirrus clouds are thin and wispy. They appear very high in the sky. Cumulus clouds are puffy. They look like cotton floating in the sky.

Skymobile

Puffy clouds can float right into your room! To make them, you will need:

Polyester fiber-fill (available at craft stores)
Scissors
White thread
White wire clothes hanger

1. Pull a few wads of fiber-fill apart and shape them into clouds of various shapes and sizes by pulling and fluffing.

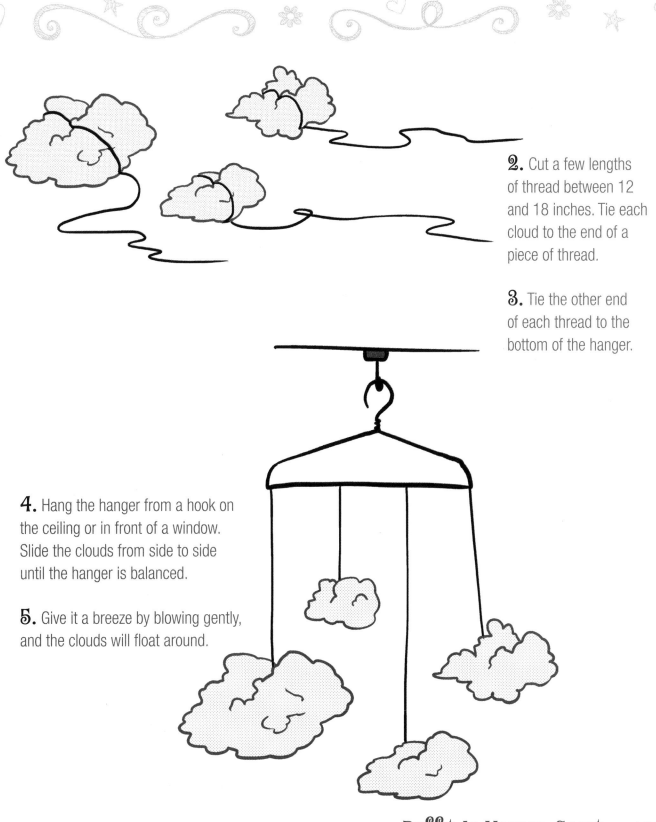

2. Cut a few lengths of thread between 12 and 18 inches. Tie each cloud to the end of a piece of thread.

3. Tie the other end of each thread to the bottom of the hanger.

4. Hang the hanger from a hook on the ceiling or in front of a window. Slide the clouds from side to side until the hanger is balanced.

5. Give it a breeze by blowing gently, and the clouds will float around.

Draw Puffit!

You're a kawaii master by now, so it's going to be as easy as floating on a cloud to draw our cute puffy friend, Puffit. Plus, Puffit is a cloud, so you can't possibly make a mistake, because clouds come in any shape. Follow these guidelines to learn to draw Puffit, and then use your kawaii technique on your own paper to draw Hamsta, Monchacha, and more of your own original cuties.

1.

2.

3.

4.

Artshmallows

Marshmallows can do more than float around in hot cocoa, you know. They can be art supplies that serve as snacks while you're making a masterpiece.

White paper
Colored mini-marshmallows
Regular-sized white marshmallows

Glue
Scissors

1. On a piece of paper, arrange a rainbow of colored mini marshmallows on your paper. At either end of the rainbow, arrange white marshmallows to form clouds.

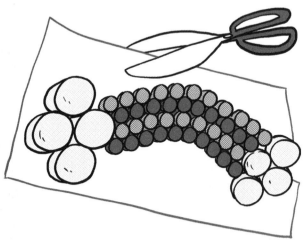

2. Once you're happy with your layout, glue each marshmallow in place. After the glue is dry, cut off the excess paper.

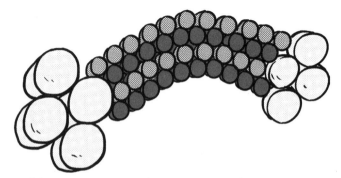

3. Hang your artshmallows on the fridge with a stick-on magnet, or pin your masterpiece up with a straight pin or thumbtack. You can even glue marshmallows to the back of the paper to make a standing rainbow centerpiece.

Chapter 14

It's Kawaii-Time We All Get Together

Now that you've gotten to know each kawaii character and had tons of fun, it's time to party! Call all your friends for a kawaii get together, and don't forget to play some silly games, make more stuff, and bask in the cute-itude of kawaii.

Kawaii-ify Your Friends

School pictures can be cute . . . but they can always be cuter! Kawaii-ify your friends and family by drawing a cuter and happier kawaii face on top of their already cute and happy faces.

F.I.B. Poetry

You're a poet and you don't know it! Help complete these cute little poems.

There's not a bunny alive that is sweeta

Than our own kawaii bunny, _____.

Salad is crisp and chickens are bony.

For dessert we want ice cream, so we call

_____.

In the cute kawaii barn is a pony named Moinka,

A ducky named Doinka,

And a piggy named

_____.

Families are full of love,

Thanks to Favva and Muvva.

Their baby is a kawaii heart,

Known to us as _____.

There's one fruit that's a sweetie,

Sweeter than a cherry,

Always juicylicious,

Who goes by

_____.

Name the kawaii guitar-playing phenomenom-nom.

It's a fruity friend we fondly call _____.

Who's the little cat

Who deserves a gentle pat?

Three cheers and chee-ow-ee . . .

That kitty is _____!

What kawaii flower

Never acts gloomy?

It's our fresh and fragrant flowery friend,

_____!

When you want a buddy

That comes from a bake-o

You can count on this sweetie: _____!

Little Miss Muffet sat on her tuffet,

Which was as soft as our fluffy pal _____!

He always runs on a squeaky little wheel.

_____ doesn't get far,

But he sure likes to squeal!

Not your average monster,

She's got polka dot pockets.

In there, _____

Might have hidden toy rockets.

Find Your Kawaii Friends

Every one of your new kawaii friends' names is hidden in this word search. Their names are listed for you, but try to remember them all just from looking at their cute pictures.

BERIBERI

BLOOMI

BUNITA

HAMSTA

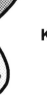

KONI

KUPKAIKO

LUVVA

MEOWY

MONCHACHA

NANANOMNOM

OINKA

PUFFIT

P	R	X	O	K	I	A	K	P	U	K	A	H
X	A	K	B	E	R	I	B	E	R	I	I	N
R	H	L	W	P	R	E	A	T	S	M	A	H
J	C	I	T	V	B	S	L	V	S	N	M	T
S	A	V	P	I	G	U	U	G	A	U	U	M
R	H	T	Y	Q	F	M	N	N	I	G	K	E
T	C	A	X	I	J	F	O	I	K	G	Q	D
O	N	K	Z	Q	I	M	U	I	T	R	O	X
O	O	N	Y	H	N	M	L	P	N	A	Y	Z
B	M	I	M	O	K	U	O	Y	W	O	E	M
K	M	O	M	X	V	Q	U	O	P	X	K	J
J	Q	S	W	V	U	A	J	K	L	Z	I	H
R	S	L	A	R	B	J	J	V	Z	B	Q	U

Kawaii Captions

Say what? Well, that's up to you. Write cute and funny captions for these adorable pictures. What's happening? You decide!

Pop for a Party with Kawaii Party Pops!

Lollipops are lovely, and they make a great party favor. Dress up some plain pops by kawaii-ifing them! You will need:

Scissors
Sticky-back foam sheets in various colors
Flat lollipops in wrappers

In addition to cute, "kawaii" can mean: lovely, charming, pretty, darling, dear, or pet.

1. Cut a circle of foam about the size of your lollipop.

2. Cut out shapes of other colors and stick them down on your circle, making the face, body, and other features of your kawaii character. The sticky-back of the foam does most of the work.

3. Place finished pops in a glass—like a sweet bouquet. Mmmmm!

Button Babies

You can make cute kawaii character jewelry from old buttons. Give it a try!
You will need:

Buttons of various shapes and colors
Glue
String
Markers

1. Dig through your buttons and find some that will go together to make a kawaii friend. It doesn't need to be a familiar friend—you can create all kinds of new characters.

2. Glue the buttons together and string the biggest one through its holes to make a necklace.

3. Add eyes and a really cute smile with markers.

Luau in the Kawaiian Islands

Now that your kawaii friends are all together, it's time to celebrate! Get some of your real-life friends together and do the limbo! The limbo is a party game that is also a dance, so put on some party music!

All you need is a broomstick or a yardstick. Two players hold the ends of the stick at about chest-height while the other players bend over backward and dance their way underneath it, trying not to touch the stick.

If anybody touches it, they're eliminated from play. After all players have taken their turn, the bar is lowered a few inches, and again, players dance underneath it from one side to the other. If you're the last player to make it under the bar without touching it . . . hooray! You win!

Answers

Carrot Cake Caper
(page 16)

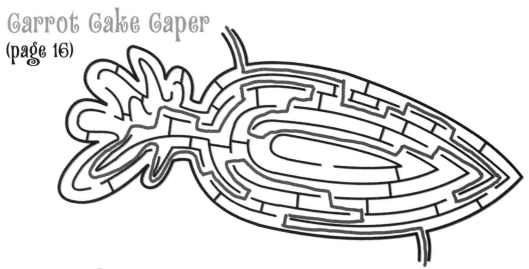

Koni's Flavor Forecast (page 23)

E	I	V	W	T	C	C	O	O	K	I	E	D	O	U	G	H	V	C
L	X	N	J	A	I	E	I	I	D	O	I	V	A	N	I	L	L	A
P	B	E	S	N	J	T	G	L	Y	R	R	E	H	C	G	N	I	B
P	M	B	C	A	B	A	M	E	C	V	Q	J	P	N	C	O	U	J
A	T	X	I	N	F	L	T	M	D	F	D	H	N	Z	R	J	S	Y
E	T	L	N	A	N	O	O	A	G	C	C	A	K	O	E	E	L	Q
N	P	Z	N	B	B	C	N	R	S	T	T	S	C	B	E	O	T	K
I	T	K	A	E	L	O	T	A	O	I	G	K	S	U	R	K	N	B
P	I	L	M	L	P	H	Z	C	L	J	Y	Z	P	T	E	I	I	W
E	H	W	O	G	E	C	S	O	K	R	P	Y	U	T	E	W	M	O
I	U	X	N	B	F	R	P	U	O	Z	R	P	M	E	B	I	R	Y
H	U	C	H	Y	E	A	Q	A	Q	R	Z	X	O	R	T	F	E	R
Y	C	A	S	T	E	K	D	H	E	B	V	J	N	B	O	N	P	R
K	Z	G	T	N	H	J	R	B	B	N	T	C	I	R	O	I	P	E
Z	Q	U	N	K	O	C	W	X	E	Z	O	N	R	I	R	E	E	E
X	B	C	B	D	D	A	A	X	F	S	B	M	R	C	I	C	P	E
L	H	D	X	Y	R	U	X	E	J	A	Y	E	E	K	T	H	L	U
R	X	S	M	T	O	N	T	U	P	U	Z	J	F	L	F	N	E	L
B	K	X	S	Y	H	G	B	N	M	U	W	Q	S	E	D	G	E	B

Sunshine and Lollipops
(page 31)

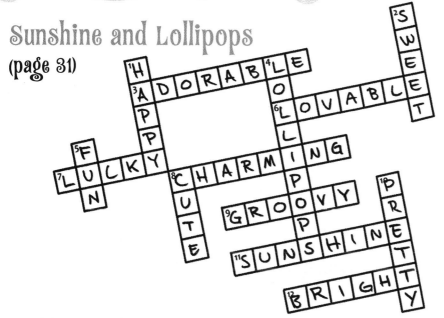

Crossword answers:
- 1 HAPPY
- 2 SWEET
- 3 ADORABLE
- 4 LOLLIPOP
- 5 FUN
- 6 LOVABLE
- 7 LUCKY
- 8 CHARMING / CUTE
- 9 GROOVY
- 10 PRETTY
- 11 SUNSHINE
- 12 BRIGHT

Tutti Fruity Duty (page 49)

Y	T	C	I	J	J	U	B	P	W	N	G	G	N	M
J	R	A	P	Z	K	Q	L	V	O	E	E	N	O	R
S	A	R	N	D	D	U	M	M	E	R	L	B	L	C
U	E	Q	E	G	M	W	E	N	U	I	P	L	E	K
P	R	P	U	B	E	L	I	T	O	X	P	I	M	X
J	J	D	A	S	W	R	V	Q	R	H	A	M	R	E
K	A	H	B	R	A	A	I	C	O	O	D	E	E	J
Y	I	P	G	T	G	L	R	N	N	N	U	I	T	V
G	O	W	C	M	B	D	D	T	E	E	R	A	A	W
V	Z	E	I	A	B	E	Z	K	S	Y	I	B	W	U
G	N	N	N	E	G	N	A	R	O	D	P	T	Q	U
X	X	A	I	H	R	B	W	G	O	E	I	N	D	M
A	N	D	D	P	E	A	C	H	G	W	V	S	T	M
A	X	E	T	A	N	A	R	G	E	M	O	P	L	Z
C	A	N	T	A	L	O	U	P	E	P	B	G	Y	I

Code Cracker (page 60)

A banana with speckles is said to have freckles.

Clueless Crossword Cruzzle (page 94)

Find Your Kawaii Friends (page 119)